HOLY CITIES

JERUSALEM

Saviour Pirotta

Dillon Press
New York

First American publication 1993 by Dillon Press,
Macmillan Publishing Company, 866 Third Avenue,
New York, NY 10022

Macmillan Publishing Company is part of the Maxwell
Communication Group of Companies.

First published by Evans Brothers Limited,
2A Portman Mansions, Chiltern Street, London W1M 1LE

Printed in Hong Kong

10 9 8 7 6 5 4 3 2 1

Library of Congress Cataloging-in-Publication Data
Pirotta, Saviour.
  Jerusalem / Saviour Pirotta.
    p. cm.—(Holy cities)
  Includes bibliographical references (p. 46) and index.
  Summary: Surveys the history, places of worship, legends,
traditions, and art and architecture of the great city, in which
Christians, Jews, and Muslims live side by side.
  ISBN 0-87518-569-X
  1. Jerusalem—History—Juvenile literature.   [1. Jerusalem.]
I. Title. II. Series.
DS109.9.P57 1993
956.94'42—dc20   92-30130

ACKNOWLEDGMENTS

Editorial: Catherine Chambers and Jean Coppendale
Design: Monica Chia
Production: Jenny Mulvanny

Maps: Jillian Luff of Bitmap Graphics

For permission to reproduce copyright material the author
and publishers gratefully acknowledge the following:

Front cover: Main photograph – The Old City of Jerusalem
– Ronald Sheridan, Ancient Art & Architecture Collection;
inset left – The Wailing Wall – Travel Photo International;
inset right – The Dome of the Rock – Sutton Promotions Ltd

Back cover: The Church of All Nations, Mount of Olives,
Jerusalem – Travel Photo International

Endpapers: Front – Christ's birthplace, Bethlehem – Douglas
Pike, Bruce Coleman Limited; Back – The interior of the
Dome of the Rock, Jerusalem – Tony Souter, The Hutchison
Picture Library

Title page: A view of old Jerusalem taken through a chapel
window on the Mount of Olives – Genut Audio Visual
Productions, Israel

Contents page: One of the artist Marc Chagall's stained-
glass windows found in the synagogue in Hadassah
Hospital – Genut Audio Visual Productions, Israel

Page 6 – Main picture – Robert Harding Picture Library,
(inset) Genut Audio Visual Productions, Israel; page 8 – (top)
Robert Harding Picture Library, (bottom) Simon McBride,
The Hutchison Picture Library; page 9 – Robert Harding
Picture Library; page 10 – Tony Souter, The Hutchison
Picture Library; page 11 – Ronald Sheridan, Ancient Art &
Architecture Collection; page 12 – Genut Audio Visual
Productions, Israel; page 13 – Genut Audio Visual
Productions, Israel; page 14 – Genut Audio Visual
Productions, Israel; page 15 – Robert Harding Picture
Library; page 16 – e.t. archive; page 17 – Ronald Sheridan,
Ancient Art & Architecture Collection; page 18 – Genut
Audio Visual Productions, Israel; page 19 – Genut Audio
Visual Productions, Israel; page 20 – Genut Audio Visual
Productions, Israel; page 21 – (top) The Hutchison Picture
Library, (bottom) Genut Audio Visual Productions, Israel;
page 22 – Ronald Sheridan, Ancient Art & Architecture
Collection; page 23 – Ronald Sheridan, Ancient Art &
Architecture Collection; page 24 – Robert Harding Picture
Library; page 25 – Genut Audio Visual Productions, Israel;
page 26 – Melanie Friend, The Hutchison Picture Library;
page 27 – Genut Audio Visual Productions, Israel; page 28 –
(left) Robert Harding Picture Library, (top) Genut Audio
Visual Productions, Israel; page 29 – (left) Robert Harding
Picture Library, (right) The Hutchison Picture Library; page
30 – Genut Audio Visual Productions, Israel; page 31 – (left)
Tony Souter, The Hutchison Picture Library, (right) F. Jack
Jackson, Robert Harding Picture Library; page 32 – (left)
Tony Souter, The Hutchison Picture Library, (top) Robert
Harding Picture Library; page 33 – Robert Harding Picture
Library; page 34 – (top) Genut Audio Visual Productions,
Israel, (bottom) Ronald Sheridan, Ancient Art & Architecture
Collection; page 35 – (bottom left) Genut Audio Visual
Productions, Israel, (inset) Robert Harding Picture Library,
(top right) Genut Audio Visual Productions, Israel; page 36 –
Genut Audio Visual Productions, Israel; page 37 – (left) T. E.
Clark, The Hutchison Picture Library, (right) Ronald
Sheridan, Ancient Art & Architecture Collection; page 38 –
Genut Audio Visual Productions, Israel; page 39 – Robert
Harding Picture Library; page 40 – Ronald Sheridan, Ancient
Art & Architecture Collection; page 41 – Robert Harding
Picture Library; page 42 – (top) Genut Audio Visual
Productions, Israel, (bottom) Tony Souter, The Hutchison
Picture Library; page 43 – Genut Audio Visual Productions,
Israel.

Contents

Jerusalem the golden

Jerusalem is one of the most fascinating cities in the world. It is a rich mixture of cultures, languages, and traditions. But more than this, it is a holy city for three of the world's largest religions: Judaism, Christianity, and Islam.

Jerusalem has been destroyed and rebuilt at least seven times throughout its long history. Its boundaries have shifted and changed repeatedly. Today, the whole city is part of the Jewish State of Israel, although people of all faiths live there.

Jerusalem's golden stone buildings are spread across a series of hills and valleys, about 2,500 feet above sea level. To the west and north, the city faces the lush, green countryside of Israel. To the east, it overlooks the scorching Judean Desert. The cool Mediterranean Sea is only about 30 miles away.

The Judean Desert stretches all the way to the ▶
Dead Sea.

Jerusalem's buildings have a rich golden glow in the early-morning and late-evening light. ▼

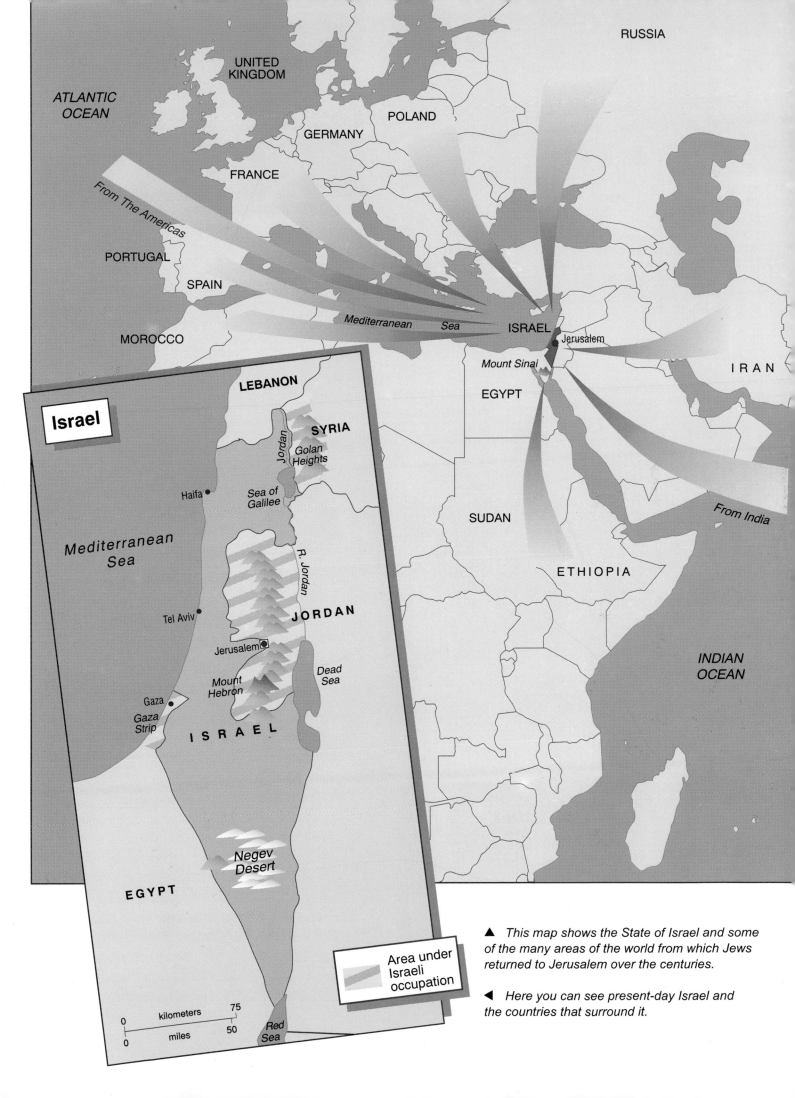

RUSSIA

UNITED
KINGDOM

ATLANTIC
OCEAN

GERMANY

POLAND

FRANCE

From The Americas

PORTUGAL

SPAIN

MOROCCO

Mediterranean   Sea

ISRAEL

Jerusalem

Mount Sinai

EGYPT

I R A N

From India

SUDAN

ETHIOPIA

INDIAN
OCEAN

Israel

LEBANON

SYRIA

Jordan

Golan
Heights

Haifa

Sea of
Galilee

Mediterranean
Sea

R. Jordan

JORDAN

Tel Aviv

Jerusalem

Dead
Sea

Mount
Hebron

Gaza

Gaza
Strip

I S R A E L

EGYPT

Negev
Desert

Area under
Israeli
occupation

▲ This map shows the State of Israel and some
of the many areas of the world from which Jews
returned to Jerusalem over the centuries.

◀ Here you can see present-day Israel and
the countries that surround it.

kilometers		75
0		
miles		50
0		

Red
Sea

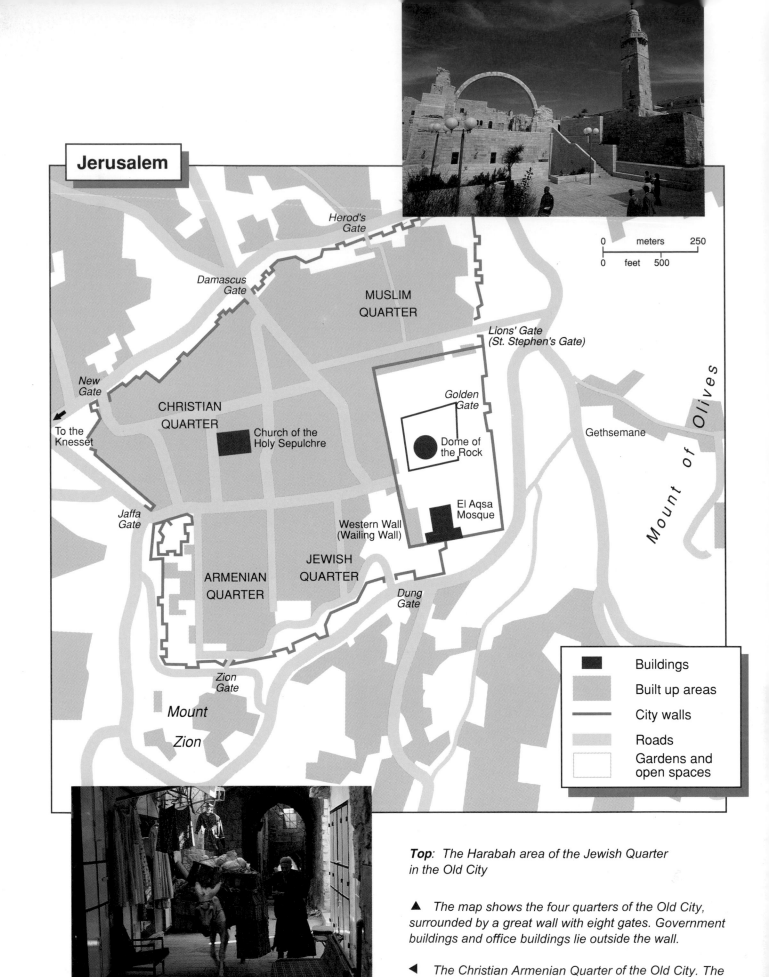

Jerusalem

Herod's Gate

Damascus Gate

MUSLIM QUARTER

Lions' Gate
(St. Stephen's Gate)

New Gate

CHRISTIAN QUARTER

Golden Gate

To the Knesset

Church of the Holy Sepulchre

Dome of the Rock

Gethsemane

El Aqsa Mosque

Jaffa Gate

Western Wall (Wailing Wall)

JEWISH QUARTER

ARMENIAN QUARTER

Dung Gate

Zion Gate

Mount Zion

Mount of Olives

0 meters 250
0 feet 500

Legend:
- Buildings
- Built up areas
- City walls
- Roads
- Gardens and open spaces

Top: The Harabah area of the Jewish Quarter in the Old City

▲ The map shows the four quarters of the Old City, surrounded by a great wall with eight gates. Government buildings and office buildings lie outside the wall.

◄ The Christian Armenian Quarter of the Old City. The Armenians have lived here for 600 years, and there are many churches and libraries in this quiet area.

A divided city

Today, Jerusalem is made up of two parts. The western part lies within the old **boundaries** of the State of Israel, which was created in 1948. This western area is called New Jerusalem because even its oldest buildings were constructed only 130 years ago. It was made the capital of Israel in 1949. Its wide streets and broad avenues run through quiet **suburbs** with new office buildings. The Knesset, the Jewish parliament, and other government buildings lie in this part. Most of the people who live in this area are Jewish.

Eastern Jerusalem is the second part and includes the Old City. The area outside the Old City is small and has fewer modern buildings than New Jerusalem. Mostly Arabs live here. Eastern Jerusalem used to be in Jordan but was made a part of Israel in 1967, after the Arab-Israeli War. The Old City is the most **densely populated** area of Jerusalem. Most of the people who live here are Christian and Muslim Arabs.

The Old City is surrounded by an ancient, high wall. Narrow, twisting streets and alleys wind around small stone houses and stores. Inside, it is divided into four quarters: Jewish, Christian, Muslim, and Armenian.

Jerusalem is a **sacred** place of **pilgrimage** for many Jews, Muslims, and Christians. Every year, thousands of pilgrims come to worship here at three of the most holy places in the world: the Jewish Wailing Wall, the Christian Church of the Holy Sepulcher, and the Muslim Dome of the Rock.

▲ Muslims have lived in the Arab Quarter for at least 800 years. The area has narrow, shady streets and street traders with market stalls. Men sit outside, playing dominoes and a local game called Shaish Baish. Backgamon

◄ Thousands of Jews have returned to Israel in the last 20 years, especially from eastern and central Europe. Many new houses like these have been built in Israel.

The people

More than 442,000 people live in Jerusalem. Of these, about 330,000 are Jewish, 100,000 are Muslim, and 12,000 are Christian. Although the official languages of Israel are Hebrew and Arabic, a visitor on a street corner of Jerusalem is likely to hear more than 70 different languages and **dialects**.

The Jews are divided in two major groups: the Ashkenazim and the Sephardim. The Ashkenazim originally came back to the Jewish homeland from the countries of eastern and central Europe, while the Sephardim are mostly the **descendants** of Jews driven from Spain in the 15th century.

There are also many other groups from western Europe and countries of the Middle East. Some Israeli Jews are from North African countries such as Morocco and from Ethiopia in northeast Africa. Cochin Jews come from India. Jewish people born in Israel are called Sabras. They form nearly half of the Jewish population.

The Christians are made up of seven main groups. Each group has its own churches: the Roman Catholic, Greek Orthodox, Armenian, Jacobite, Coptic, Syrian, and Anglican.

Most of Jerusalem's Muslims are from families who have lived in and around the city for many hundreds of years, when the country was known as Palestine. They are called Palestinian Arabs.

▲ *Two priests of the Greek Orthodox church are talking to each other by the Wailing Wall. Jerusalem was conquered by Greek-speaking Jews about 2,200 years ago. Many Jews learned the Greek language. The Torah, one of the holy books of the Jews, was translated into Greek. It was mostly Greek Jews who became the first Christians.*

Key words

boundaries   the far edges around a country that divide it from other countries

declared   announced

suburbs   areas outside a city center, where people live

densely populated   many people living in a small area

sacred   holy

pilgrimage   a special journey made to a holy place by people who go there to worship

dialects   different ways of speaking the same language

descendants   children, their children, and so on

A Global family

The 330,000 Jews living in Jerusalem make up about 2% of the worldwide Jewish community. The largest numbers of Jews live in North America (6,900,000) and Asia (5,375,000).

The birth of Jerusalem

Long before it developed into a religious center for three of the world's largest faiths, there was a small, simple settlement where Jerusalem now stands. It is hard to imagine that a third of the world's population now think of Jerusalem as a sacred city.

Archaeologists have found remains of people and their homes in this area that are 5,000 years old. The Egyptians mention in their writings that communities had developed here by 1900 BC, or about 4,000 years ago. The first small groups of people built tiny settlements in the middle of a harsh, unwelcoming landscape.

It seems impossible that anyone would want to settle here. Jerusalem sits on the edge of a desert, away from the cool sea and among rocky hills (see page 7). The secret lies in two surprising sources of water. Jerusalem rests near the Gihon spring and between the Kidron and Hinnom valleys, which catch precious rainfall. So with bubbling fresh water and fertile land, the first settlers were able to build small farming communities.

It is no wonder that Jerusalem and the land in which it grew seem blessed by God. But sometimes people fight over blessings, and Jerusalem, with all its riches, suffered some 30 long, hard battles. Many of these were between the Jews, Christians, and Muslims, who all, at one time or another, claimed the city and the country around it. It therefore seems strange that these religions share the same origins, many of the same **prophets**, and the belief in one God.

Jerusalem, the dream

The life of Abraham, and of the people who followed him, became the first part of the story of Jerusalem as a holy city. There is very little proof that this story is true. But it is believed by millions of people all over the world and is at the heart of their faith in one God.

The story of Abraham and his descendants is told in the **TeNaKah**, the holy Bible of the Jews. It appears in the Old Testament of the Christian Bible and was **revealed** to the Prophet Muhammad, as written down in the

The fertile valleys to the north, west, and south of Jerusalem often have terraces, or steps, made into the hillsides for growing crops or trees. Almonds, olives, and ▼ figs have been grown here for thousands of years.

Koran, the **sacred** book of the Muslims. The books all tell the story in a different way, and the followers of each religion respect the one they are familiar with.

Around 4,000 years ago, Abraham dreamed of a rich, green land, just like the valleys of Kidron and Hinnom. He and his family lived far away in a city called Ur, in Mesopotamia. The dream led him and his family to drive their flocks of sheep toward Canaan in Palestine. It is believed that they stopped at a small settlement that later became Jerusalem, although none of the holy books actually mentions this.

It was here that God tested Abraham's faith in him. Abraham was asked to **sacrifice** his only son, Isaac. It is thought that he prepared to kill Isaac on Mount Moriah, where the Old City of Jerusalem now stands. God was satisfied with the strength of Abraham's faith and stopped the sacrifice from taking place. The Dome of the Rock now covers the spot where this event is believed to have happened.

Isaac's son was named Jacob. Jacob's twelve sons raised twelve large families, or **tribes**. The Jews, who came from Judah, were one of these tribes. The twelve tribes suffered many hardships and threats throughout their history. They were forced into **exile** by drought and by war.

One of the Hebrew leaders, Moses, led them back to Canaan from exile in Egypt. God told the Hebrews that they would be given their Promised Land, but on condition that Moses and his people obeyed God's laws. Among the many hundreds of laws that God made, the Ten Commandments were the most important. They were written on two stone tablets, and Moses made a wooden box for them called the Ark of the Covenant.

The Ark of the Covenant is thought to be buried under layers of building and rubble on Mount Moriah. These laws and many other commandments were later written down in the Torah. All synagogues, or Jewish places of worship, have their own ark, in which the writings of the Torah are kept.

Kings and palaces

The people of Israel became united, or joined together, by King Saul. But it was King David who fought for the small town of Jebus, which afterward became known as Jerusalem, the City of Peace. David turned Jerusalem into a religious city—a home for the Ark of the Covenant. But the City of Peace later turned into a city of battle and destruction.

King Solomon, who came to the throne in 968 BC, made Jerusalem into an important, bustling city. He built himself magnificent palaces and a beautiful temple in which to

◀ *Each synagogue has a Torah scroll like this one. Beautiful scarves have been draped around the sides. A brightly colored cloth covers the Torah when it is closed, although during the bar mitzvah ceremony it is changed to a white one (see page 25).*

keep the Ark. Enormous golden stones and cedarwood from Lebanon were used to create the splendid city.

From this time Jerusalem developed as an economic center. Traders came from across the mountains and deserts of the Middle East. But its riches and importance, and its position between the eastern and Mediterranean countries, only made Jerusalem an even greater target for jealousy and greed. The city was torn apart and rebuilt again and again over the centuries. The broken ruins have proved that many of the stories of Saul, David, and Solomon, written in the holy books, are true.

This is the Citadel and Tower of King David, who had to attack the strong fortifications of Mount Zion before he
▼ *could enter Jerusalem.*

Key words

BC before the birth of Christ

prophets religious people who are believed to have been given messages by God; they were teachers and preachers who told people how God wanted them to live

TeNaKah the Torah, Neviim, and Ketuvim holy books

revealed shown

tribe groups of people joined together to form a community

sacrifice to kill something or somebody as a sign of obedience to gods or a god

exile a person who is forced to live outside his or her own country

The Sacred Ark

The Ark of the Covenant is said to possess mysterious powers. At the battle of Jericho, priests carried it around the city seven times and the walls collapsed. Treasure seekers have tried to find the Ark for centuries, hoping to learn its secrets.

Sharing Jerusalem

Jews, Christians, and Muslims have been drawn to Jerusalem by the stories of Abraham, which they share. But each religion has its own special link with Jerusalem that it cannot share with the others.

Jerusalem for the Jews

Jerusalem became special to the Jews as the city that was built by them for the glory of God and as the center of their religion and culture.

Over the centuries, Jews were forced to scatter to many parts of the world (see page 22). But the Jewish religion did not die. Religious men who had been pushed out of Jerusalem began to write down teachings, telling Jews how they should live and worship, which were set down in a book called the Talmud. These writings kept the Jewish religion and way of life alive in many different parts of the world.

By following the teachings in the Torah and the Talmud, Jews prepared themselves for the day when they would return to Jerusalem. Rabbis, or teachers, in many different countries helped to keep alive and strengthen the Jewish faith and culture. For

▲ *This is a model of the well-planned palace built by King Herod the Great.*

many hundreds of years the Jewish people waited for the time when they could return to Jerusalem.

Today, Jews no longer have to hope and pray for their return to the Promised Land. Now they long for the day when God will send the Messiah, a chosen leader, to make the whole world a perfect place to live in.

Jerusalem for the Christians

The Jews had been conquered and **oppressed** by many peoples. In 63 BC the Romans became their new rulers. In 37 BC they made a local man king of Judea, the Romans' new name for the country around Jerusalem. The ruler's name was Herod the Great, and he was disliked by the Jews, who prayed that one day a holy person would come to save them from oppression. They called this holy person the Messiah. As we know already, Jews today are still waiting for him to come.

The talk of a Messiah alarmed Herod, who was afraid that he would want to take Herod's place as ruler. One day, three wise men came to see him. They told him that the

◀ *Schoolchildren listen carefully while the rabbi reads from the Torah.*

Savior, a new king, had just been born, and that they had come from their own lands to worship him. Herod acted quickly. He sent his soldiers to kill every newborn baby in the land. The soldiers carried out his horrific command. But one baby managed to escape with his parents to Egypt. This baby's name was Jesus of Nazareth.

When Jesus grew up, he returned to Judea, not to save the Jews from the Romans, but to tell people about God's love for them and about how they must try to be kind and loving. Many of the Jewish leaders were jealous of Jesus. When he went to Jerusalem to celebrate the Jewish feast of the Passover (see page 34), he was cheered and paraded through the streets by hundreds of Jews. The jealous Jews plotted against him. The Roman governor of Judea, Pontius Pilate, sent Jesus to the ruler of Galilee and Perea, Herod

Antipas, son of Herod the Great, for judgment. But in the end it was Pilate himself who **tried** Jesus and sentenced him to death.

He was taken outside Jerusalem to a hill called Golgotha and nailed to a wooden cross. His followers wept at his death. Christians believe that Jesus rose from the dead after three days, and later went up to heaven to be with God.

The teachings of Jesus Christ, his death, and his resurrection are central teachings of the Christian faith. Jesus spent those last important days of his life on Earth in Jerusalem, so it is not surprising that Christians come as pilgrims to this holy city.

Life has not changed much for these nomads since ancient times. Most of the nomads in Israel and the ▼ *countries around it are Muslims (see page 16).*

Jerusalem for the Muslims

Muslims are the followers of the Holy Prophet Muhammad, who was born around AD 570 in the city of Mecca. He was a member of the ruling Quraysh tribe. His family has been trace back to Abraham. Muhammad's father died shortly before his birth, so the boy was raised by his uncles in the desert.

When he grew up, Muhammad traveled as a **merchant** all over the desert, where he met and talked with many people. Some of these people were Jews and Christians who lived in small communities in different parts of the desert.

At this time, Arabs worshiped many gods. People came every year to the city of Mecca from all over the desert to worship the gods at a holy shrine, called the Kaaba. Muhammad did not like this. He wanted to be like Abraham, the Jews, and the Christians, and worship only one god. One night, while praying in a cave, Muhammad saw the

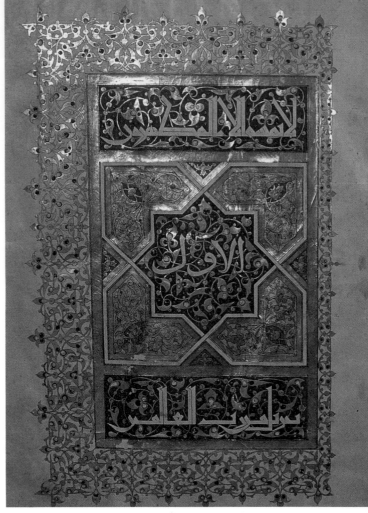

archangel Gabriel, who gave him a message from God. This and later messages formed the teachings of the Holy Koran, the book by which all the followers of Muhammad live.

Many people joined the Holy Prophet in his new religion. They became known as Muslims, which means "they who surrender to God." Their faith was called Islam, and all followers were told in the Holy Koran to live according to five rules. These are the Five Pillars of Faith, which are: to declare a belief in God and in Muhammad as his messenger, to pray five times each day, to **fast**, to give to the poor, and to make at least one **pilgrimage** to Mecca.

◀ *The Kaaba shrine in Mecca is the most important place for Muslims to visit on their pilgrimages. Here you can see pilgrims walking around the Kaaba. They must do this seven times. The men are wearing their special pilgrimage dress called* ihram. *Women have their heads covered but must not wear a veil over their faces. Children and invalids also try to complete the pilgrimage.*

This beautiful Koran with gold Arabic script, or writing, was made nearly 1,300 years ago.

even though he described a **caravan** he saw on the way there. But there were those who did believe him. From then on, Jerusalem became a holy city for Muslims, the third most important after Mecca and Medina. Muslims believe that on the final day of the world, the day of the Last Judgment, God will descend to Jerusalem on black clouds, while Jesus judges the dead.

Key words

oppressed   not treated well or allowed to live freely

tried   judged in a court of law

AD   the years after Christ was born

merchant   trader—someone who sells goods

archangel   one of the chief angels

fast   to go without food for a certain length of time

pilgrimage   a visit to a holy place where people pray and perform special rituals

persecuting   being cruel

caravan   a group of people who travel together for safety, especially merchants

Inside the Kaaba

According to Islamic tradition, the Kaaba was built by Abraham and Ishmael, the fathers of the Muslim faith. The shrine is sacred because it houses the Black Stone, said to have been given to Abraham by the archangel Gabriel. The Black Stone sits in the eastern corner of the Kaaba.

The leaders of Mecca did not like the new religion. They were afraid that people would stop coming to their city to worship at the Kaaba. These pilgrims always brought trade, and therefore money, to Mecca. So the leaders started **persecuting** the Muslims, who in the end had to flee to the city of Medina.

It is said that one night, while sleeping in a house in Mecca, Muhammad was awakened by the archangel Gabriel. The archangel had brought a curious beast with him. The legend is that it was smaller than a mule and taller than an ass. Best of all, it could gallop faster than lightning. It was called Buraq.

Muhammad mounted the beast and in a second he was taken to Jerusalem, where he sat on the holy rock upon which the Jewish king Solomon had built his temple. Slowly Muhammad rose to the heavens. There he talked to Adam, Abraham, Moses, and Jesus.

On his quick return to Mecca, Muhammad told his followers all about his sacred journey. Some people did not believe him,

Jerusalem lost

After the reign of King Solomon, some Jews began to worship other gods, and leaders argued with one another over the way in which Israel should be ruled. Jerusalem became weak, and over the next 2,000 years the city faced wave upon wave of attack, destruction, and rebuilding.

The layers of different stonework and the styles of architecture that can be seen today in ancient buildings show that Jerusalem was once part of many different **empires**.

The first battle for Jerusalem

The tribes of Israel, to the north of Jerusalem, were the first Jewish peoples to be attacked, and their towns and cities were destroyed when the Assyrians overran their kingdom in 722 BC. The people fled to many different parts of the world. The descendants of many of these people have returned to the Jewish homeland during the last 50 years.

Jerusalem itself survived until 587 BC, when Nebuchadnezzar, king of Babylon,

▲ *A menorah is being lit as part of the Hanukkah celebrations (see page 34).*

invaded Jerusalem, leaving it for the next ruler, Zedekiah, to **raze** it completely to the ground in 588 BC. Solomon's wonderful temple was burned down and most of the city's mansions and palaces were destroyed.

The Jews managed to regain their city twice during the constant change of rulers. The first time, a new but smaller temple was completed in 515 BC. But many of the old Jewish buildings and palaces were never restored. Jerusalem was then ruled by other kingdoms and empires. The Greek rulers of this holy city in the 4th century BC gave way to Egyptian and Seleucid (Syrian) rulers.

The Jews regained Jerusalem for a second time when the Seleucid rulers were driven out by the Maccabean Jews in the 2d century BC. They were led by a man called Mattathias and his sons, the Maccabees. The Jewish religion was restored and the Jewish temple was **reconsecrated** in 164 BC, with much joy

◄ *This ancient stone carving was found in Ashkelon, about 37 miles from Jerusalem. It shows the Egyptian goddess Isis, with Horus, her child.*

and happiness. The Jews still celebrate the rededication of the temple in a festival called Hanukkah.

This was the last time that Jerusalem was the holy city for the Jews, apart from four years between AD 66 and AD 70, when they attacked their new Roman rulers and captured the city.

Romans in Jerusalem

In AD 70 the Romans returned, murdered most of the Jews, and destroyed Herod's magnificent temple, his beautiful palace, the theater, and many houses. Jerusalem was left in ruins for 60 years.

A new Roman ruler, Hadrian, returned in the 2d century AD. He decided to build a new city on top of the old one. The new town was to be a colony, a Roman city with many officers to look after their conquered land. The Jews tried unsuccessfully to rebel against the Romans between AD 132 and 135. Afterward they were forbidden to live in Jerusalem. But some entered quietly and made their homes there anyway.

▲ *These remains are the Kardo—a wide Roman town with arches, **colonnades**, and a **forum**. When Hadrian was ruler, temples for the Roman gods were built, and a theater and two public baths were opened.*

By this time Christianity had made small beginnings as a new religion. At first, Christians worshiped like Jews in the synagogues. But then they started meeting in their own churches. The Romans made life as awful for the Christians as they did for the Jews.

The Christian city of Jerusalem

In AD 313, things changed for the Christians. The Roman emperor Constantine supported them. The Romans now called the city of Jerusalem Aelia Capitolina. It was made part of Constantine's Christian empire.

Helena, Constantine's mother and a very religious woman, traveled to the Holy Land to visit Christ's tomb. There she discovered the cross on which she believed that Jesus was hanged, in a cave near Golgotha, just outside Jerusalem. A magnificent church was built on the spot. Part of the cross was put inside it. It became known as the Church of the Holy Sepulcher, and pilgrims from all over the world flocked to Jerusalem to

◄ *Gold coins made after the Maccabean rebellion to show that Jerusalem belonged once more to the Jews.*

worship and pray at the Christian **shrines**. Later, many more chapels were put up to mark important religious places.

Jerusalem remained one of the most important and the most magnificent cities in the world for the next 300 years. Then, in AD 614, the Persians attacked Judea. The small Jewish community decided to help them to capture Jerusalem. In a matter of days, the city was reduced to rubble once more. The relic of the cross was carried away and the city's rulers were taken prisoner.

A few years later, the Christians pushed out the Persians. Heraclius, the Christian emperor, ordered all Jews to leave Jerusalem, or they would be killed. The relic of the cross was returned to its special place in the city.

Slowly, the Christians started to rebuild the city. But the long war with the Persians had left them exhausted. In AD 636, when the Muslims, from the growing Arab Empire, appeared, the Christians just gave in.

The Islamic city of Jerusalem

By the beginning of the 7th century, most of the countries around Palestine had converted to Islam, the religion of the Muslims, the followers of Muhammad. In 638, a Muslim caliph, or leader, called Omar arrived and decided to make Jerusalem a Muslim city.

The city was so weak that he did not have to fight for it. Omar entered Jerusalem on a

▲ *This Byzantine map of Jerusalem was made nearly 1,700 years ago. It is a mosaic, a picture made from tiny pieces of colored tile, glass, or other material.*

camel. No soldiers accompanied him, just a servant carrying a day's supply of dates.

The caliph allowed the Christians to remain in Jerusalem and to worship at the various shrines and churches. The Jews were also allowed back into the city. But everyone had to pay a tax to stay there.

About fifty years later, one of Omar's **successors** decided to make Jerusalem a Muslim place of pilgrimage, like Mecca. He built a huge dome over the sacred rock and had it covered in gold.

The Muslim rulers who followed Omar were not as kind to the Christians and the Jews. Many were not allowed to pray at the Church of the Holy Sepulcher, or the Wailing Wall.

The Crusades

Muslim rule over Jerusalem lasted until the 11th century. In 1099, the leaders of the

◄ *This is thought to be the site of Christ's tomb in the Church of the Holy Sepulcher.*

This confusion of peoples, cultures, and religions made Jerusalem one of the most fascinating and mysterious cities in the world. But what happened to the Jews themselves during all this time?

Key words

empire many countries that are under the rule of just one country

raze destroy completely

reconsecrated made holy again through a special ceremony

colonnade a row of columns

forum a meeting place, usually a large square surrounded by buildings

shrine a special place where a holy person lived or visited or is buried

successor someone who follows a person in a job or position

massacre the killing of many people together in one place

Western Christian church decided to stop the spread of Islam throughout the world. With the blessing of the pope, the leader of the Roman Catholic church, Christian soldiers went to wage war against the Muslims in Palestine. These wars were known as the Crusades. The word *Crusade* comes from *cross*, the symbol of Christianity.

People from all over Europe joined the Holy Crusade on its way to Jerusalem. The Crusaders entered the city and destroyed it on the second attack. In a horrible **massacre** that shocked even the Christians in faraway countries, thousands of Muslims and Jews were killed.

The Crusaders built more than 60 churches and shrines. But their rule lasted only until 1187, when Saladin, a Turkish Muslim leader, captured the city again. Jerusalem remained mainly in the hands of Muslims until 1918, after the Turks were defeated in the First World War.

The Crusaders built these pillars, which are at the ▶ entrance to the Church of the Holy Sepulcher.

The Diaspora–the scattering

The word *Diaspora* is used to describe how most of the Jews split into different groups and journeyed throughout Asia, North Africa, and Europe, mainly as a result of different **conquests** of their homeland. Some of the invaders of Jerusalem murdered Jews or sent them into exile.

When the Babylonians destroyed Jerusalem in 588 BC, they actually took thousands of Jews to Babylon, leaving only the poorest in the holy city. But when the Greeks, under Alexander the Great, entered Jerusalem in the 4th century BC, the Jews were not harmed or driven out. Many just took advantage of the enormous empire that Alexander had created in the lands around the Mediterranean Sea. They traveled freely to other countries, where they settled.

It was the Jewish exiles in Babylon who strengthened the ideas of Jerusalem as the spiritual center for the Jews and Israel as their Holy Land. Scribes began to write down in books the traditions and history of the Jews and the teachings of the prophets. These books became honored and studied by Jews in exile. Prayer meetings took place in people's homes, as there was no Temple to worship in. Families became important in keeping the Jewish religion and way of life alive.

A prophet called Isaiah prepared the Jews for their new life in Jerusalem. His words came true when the Persians conquered Babylon and allowed the Jews to return to Jerusalem. Not all of Jerusalem was rebuilt, but in 516 BC the Second Temple was completed. All aspects of life became organized according to religious laws. The scribes and teachers later completed the scriptures, or holy books.

In later centuries, scribes explained the teachings of the TeNaKah. Their writings are known as the Talmud.

When Jews were later forced into exile again, they took with them an organized religion. Wherever they went, or wherever they were sent, they were able to worship in family groups or small communities according to their holy books. But each year, during the feast of the Passover, Jewish communities throughout the world would celebrate the time when Moses led the Israelites out of Egypt. At the Passover meals, the head of each family would say, *"Le shana haba bi Yerushalaim,"* which is Hebrew for "Next year in Jerusalem". They always longed for their Promised Land and their sacred city, Jerusalem.

▲ *A family is celebrating Passover at the special* seder *table. The family eats certain foods and says prayers.*

Key words

conquests   defeats in battle

Zionism–a nation for the Jews

Jews return to Palestine

Small groups of Jews managed to stay in Palestine, and in Jerusalem, throughout the centuries, even though mostly Muslim Arabs and some Christians lived there. Other Jews gradually returned to join them.

By 1914, there were 85,000 Jews living in Palestine. When the Turks left the area after they were defeated in the First World War in 1918, the Jews asked for their own homeland in Palestine.

The British had been given the job of ruling Palestine after the end of the war. They knew that the Muslim community had lived here for many hundreds of years. This was the home of the Palestinians, who were threatened by the idea of a Jewish nation. So the British refused to give the Jews their own homeland.

Zionism outside Palestine

Zion was a symbol of struggle and triumph for Jews. It was the fortress that King David had to conquer before he could enter Jebus many centuries before (see pages 12 and 13).

Since 1896, a man named Theodor Herzl, from Eastern Europe, had been getting other Jews interested in what he called Zionism—making a country in Palestine for all Jews so that they could live together without fear. The Jews within Palestine and those scattered throughout the world were trying to establish a land for their people.

In 1922 Jews were allowed to buy land in Palestine. This did not work, as the Muslim Palestinians and the Jews fought over it. A lot of fighting followed, and in 1947 the United Nations made a plan to divide Palestine into Jewish and Muslim countries. They wanted Jerusalem to become an **international** city. This was so that people of all religions could

▲ *Many buildings such as these were destroyed during the Six Day War.*

enter it and worship freely at the holy places.

But in the spring of 1948, Jews and Muslims rejected the idea of dividing the land of Palestine into two countries, and a bitter war was fought. In the end, Israel gained the western part of Jerusalem, and the eastern part was gained by the Muslim Transjordan government. In 1949 the New City of Western Jerusalem was made the capital of Israel.

Since then, life has been uneasy between Jews and Arabs in this area. There has been a lot of violence. In 1967, after the Six Day War between Israel and several Muslim countries, Israel at last gained the whole of the city of Jerusalem for the Jewish people.

Key words

international   belonging to more than one country

Jewish places of worship

The Jewish Wailing Wall

Jerusalem holds the most important holy place for Jews all over the world. This is the Western Wall, usually called the Wailing Wall. It is thought to be the only part of Herod's Temple still left standing after the destruction of Jerusalem in AD 70. It actually stretches from one end of Temple Mount to the other, but most of it is buried under rubble. Beneath the ruins of Herod's Temple, and many layers of other buildings, is what is left of the Temple of Solomon. Many Jews believe that the Ark of the Covenant still lies inside the ruined Temple in the Holy of Holies, a place where only the high priest could go. This makes the Wailing Wall a very special, sacred place.

Jews used to come to Temple Mount to weep about the destruction of the First Temple and to pray that Jerusalem would become their city again. When the Aqsa (pronounced "Aksa") Mosque and the Dome of the Rock were built by Muslims on Temple Mount, the wall became the only place where Jews could show their sadness. There is a legend among Jews that the drops of morning dew on the wailing Wall are the tears of the children of Israel that were shed when the Temple was destroyed.

Today, the Western Wall and the whole of Jerusalem are part of the State of Israel. Jews no longer come to the wall to weep. Instead they come to pray and to celebrate. Many people write prayers and wishes on pieces of paper and stuff them in the spaces between the enormous stones, called ashlars. Others come to read from their weekly portion of the Torah, the Jewish holy scriptures. Everyone who approaches the wall must be suitably dressed. Men wear head coverings and women cover their shoulders, even when it is very hot.

In 1967, after the Six Day War, the land surrounding the Wailing Wall was cleared to make space for all the visitors and tourists, as well as for festivals and celebrations. Many houses that were built against the wall were knocked down.

A place for celebration

When a girl is twelve years old and a boy is thirteen, their parents hold a special ceremony for them. It marks what is called the coming of age. Afterward, these children are expected to be more responsible for their

▲ *Bar mitzvah is a time for celebration at the Wailing Wall. This boy will now be able to read the Torah by himself to the rest of the congregation in the synagogue.*

own actions. The ceremony for girls is called *bas mitzvah*, or "daughter of the commandment." The ceremony for boys is known as *bar mitzvah*, or "son of the commandment."

Some parents like to hold the bar mitzvah festivities at the Wailing Wall. They take place there every week on a Monday or Thursday. In families that keep strict, or Orthodox, traditions only boys can take part in the bar mitzvah ceremony. In those families with more modern, or Reform, ideas, both boys and girls can share the same **rituals** and celebrations.

Synagogues

Over many hundreds of years, small groups of Jews returned to their holy city from other parts of the world. The settlers soon began to build synagogues. Many of these places of worship showed the styles and customs of the lands that the Jews had left behind.

Rambam Synagogue

One synagogue that still stands today was built by a man called Rambam, a Jew who had returned from Spain. He built it with the tiny community that had remained in Palestine throughout all the suffering. These Jews were finally allowed to build a synagogue in the 13th century AD. It was

People worshiping inside part of the Yohanan Ben
▼ *Zakkai Synagogue*

▲ *It is normal to see Orthodox Jews in traditional dress walking through the streets of Mea Shearim. Visitors to this area must wear clothing that covers the body well.*

Sephardic Jews and was their main place of worship for hundreds of years. A lot of it was destroyed in the war in 1967, so it has been decorated with works of art brought from synagogues in Italy, where many centuries ago there was a large Jewish community.

The Ashkenazim Jews (see page 10) used to pray in the Yehuda He-Hasid Synagogue. This grand building was started in 1699, when a thousand Polish Jews followed Rabbi Yehuda to Jerusalem and settled there. It was finished in 1864 and was the center of Ashkenazim worship for many years. But the original building was reduced to ruins in the war of 1967.

The Jerusalem Great Synagogue

The Jerusalem Great Synagogue, which was opened in 1983, is situated in West Jerusalem. It is used for festivals as well as for worship on Saturday, the Sabbath, or special day of worship. God told Moses to keep this day of the week holy, a law that most Jews obey.

Close to this synagogue is the district of Mea Shearim, which means One Hundred Gates. This is the home of the Orthodox Jews, who live according to strict religious rules. Pilgrims to this place must observe the customs of the local people. Women must cover their heads and wear long skirts. On the Sabbath, daily life comes to a complete halt as people flock to the many synagogues in the area.

Worship in a synagogue

Jews worship a lot in their own homes, where many ceremonies and celebrations take place. But on the Sabbath, Jews go to the synagogue to take part in a service. Each service is led by a rabbi, who is both a teacher and a religious leader. Rabbis are free to choose what to preach to their **congregations**. But they do have to make sure that a certain part of the Torah is read each week. A special prayer is offered to God when the Torah scroll is taken from its ark in each synagogue. The prayer

named Rambam Synagogue and was built in the southeast part of the Old City, later known as the Jewish Quarter.

Until this synagogue was built, it was not easy for Jews to hold prayer meetings. This was because there had to be at least ten men gathered together before a meeting could take place. The community was so small that finding enough men at the right time was difficult. But the problem was solved by the new synagogue because it attracted more Jews to Jerusalem. As these people settled down, the area developed and became known as the Jewish Quarter.

Yohanan Ben Zakkai Synagogue

There are many ancient synagogues in Jerusalem. One of these, the Yohanan Ben Zakkai Synagogue, is actually four synagogues in one. It was built in 1586 by

▲ Dressed in skullcaps and prayer shawls, these young Jewish boys are reading from the Torah at school.

Inside the Yad Vashem Museum of the Holocaust ▶ there are many horrifying pictures of ill-treated, starved Jewish prisoners.

ends with these words: "Father of compassion, may it be thy will to favor Zion with thy goodness and rebuild the walls of Jerusalem. For in thee alone do we trust, O King, high and exalted God, Lord of the universe."

Yad Vashem

In West Jerusalem there is a memorial to the six million Jews killed in Nazi death camps during the Second World War. It is called Yad Vashem and sits on the Mount of Remembrance. Inside there are exhibitions and written records that show what happened during this time, which is known as the Holocaust. A **mosaic** floor bears the names of the 21 concentration camps in which the Jews died. Although this is not a religious shrine, people often leave Yad Vashem saddened but strengthened.

Key words

rituals special actions or ceremonies, part of a ceremony

congregation a gathering of people for worship

mosaic a picture or writings made up of thousands of tiny pieces of colored stone or other material

Christian shrines and churches

A pilgrimage to Jerusalem can be a very busy time for a Christian. There are many churches and shrines to visit, as well as various rituals to perform.

Churches

The Church of the Holy Sepulcher is the most important Christian shrine in Jerusalem. It is made up of various chapels, which belong to six different Christian groups. These chapels spread across the sites of Christ's crucifixion and resurrection. The church has been a place of pilgrimage since early in Christianity's history.

The **foundation stone** was set in AD 326, when Empress Helena, mother of the Roman emperor Constantine, is said to have discovered a piece of the cross in a cave by the hill on which the church is built. For years, the church was the most splendid in all the world. But in AD 614, it was destroyed by the Persians. The Crusaders built most of the present building in 1149, although fires and earthquakes have meant that parts have had to be rebuilt.

On the evening before Good Friday, the day when Jesus was crucified, many people visit the church to take part in a special ceremony. The day before Christ died, he invited his special followers, the apostles, to a meal now called the Last Supper. On this

▲ **Monks** are praying in the chapel built over Calvary, where Jesus was hung on the cross.

day, known as Maundy, or Holy, Thursday, Christ asked the apostles to spread his teachings and do many things for him. The word *maundy* means "command."

Before the meal, Christ washed his apostles' feet. He told these chosen men that they must wash the feet of the poor to remind themselves of Him. So every year on Maundy Thursday, in the Catholic church, the priest humbly bathes his priests' feet. In the afternoon, the Coptic Christians, who were originally from Egypt, have a similar celebration in their chapel above the Holy Sepulcher. Their leading priest touches the hands and foreheads of his congregation with holy water.

◀ These clustered domes and towers all belong to the Church of the Holy Sepulcher.

Another group of Christians, the Abyssinians, originally from Ethiopia, perform the same ritual on top of a beautiful chapel called Saint Helena's. This is also part of the Church of the Holy Sepulcher. The Abyssinian priest washes the feet of his entire congregation in water scented with bay leaves.

Meanwhile, the Armenian Christians, who were originally from western Asia, have their service in the ancient Cathedral of Saint James. The Anglicans, members of the Church of England, have a simpler service in Saint George's Cathedral. At sunset, the Syrian Christians cram into the little church of Saint Mark to watch their patriarch, or priest, wash the feet of thirteen priests and **laymen** who represent the apostles.

The Church of the Holy Sepulcher is governed by many different Christian **denominations**. Sometimes they cannot agree with one another over the care of the church, so important **restoration** work has been left undone and the buildings need a lot of repair. There is an old wooden ladder that rests against one of the walls of the church. It has been there for years because no one can agree on who owns it!

The Via Dolorosa

On Good Friday, many pilgrims retrace Christ's footsteps from Herod's palace, where he was condemned to death, to his tomb in the Church of the Holy Sepulcher. This walk is called the Via Dolorosa: the walk of sorrow. There are 14 stops on the way, which the faithful call holy stations. These are thought to be places where Christ himself stopped or where certain things happened to him on the way to his crucifixion. These stations include the spot where Christ was stripped and beaten and the chapel built on the site where a woman wiped his face with a piece of cloth. Legend tells that an image of Christ's face remained on the cloth.

At each station the faithful stop to pray. Some carry a cross along the way as a sign of deep respect. At the final station, in Christ's tomb, the pilgrims stop to look at the marble slab on which Christ's body is thought to have been laid.

▲ *On Good Friday, crowds of people take part in the walk along the Via Dolorosa. Some people carry a cross, as Christ did.*

As many Christians cannot visit Jerusalem during Easter, the holy walk along the Via Dolorosa does not take place only on Good Friday. Franciscan monks organize a small pilgrimage every Friday, and some people walk the route whenever they can.

Other churches

One of the most-loved Christian shrines is the Basilica of the Agony. It was built in 1924 and stands in the Garden of Gethsemane, the olive grove where Christ prayed on the night before his death. Some people call it the Church of All Nations because Christians from all over the world helped to build it by sending money.

There is another church in the Garden of Gethsemane. It is called the Russian Orthodox Church of Mary Magdalene. Mary Magdalene was a follower of Jesus. Her church has beautiful onion-shaped domes and was built about 100 years ago by order of the Russian czar Alexander the Third, in memory of his mother. It is maintained by Russian Orthodox **nuns**.

A few steps away from Gethsemane, pilgrims can also visit Mary's tomb. Mary was the mother of Jesus. Some Christians believe that she did not die, but that she fell asleep and then followed her son up to heaven, body and soul. For centuries, pilgrims have come here to pray and to light scented **votive candles**. The walls of the tomb are black with smoke.

Worship in a church

The special holy day for Christians each week is Sunday. Services are led by a priest or minister, who chooses hymns, psalms, and prayers to praise and worship God. The most important prayer is the Lord's Prayer, which Christ told all his followers to say every day. Christians also say a creed, in which they declare their belief in God and in Jesus Christ. Christians take part in Mass or Holy Communion. In this ceremony, a priest or minister gives each member of the church a little bread and wine. At the Last Supper, Christ asked the apostles to do this to remind them of him. The bread represents Christ's body, and the wine, his blood. Some Christians believe that the bread and wine actually transform, or change, into the body and blood of Christ.

▲ The Russian Orthodox Church of Mary Magdalene was built in 1888. Inside there is a room in which lie the remains of a grand duchess killed during the Russian Revolution.

▲ The beautiful Church of All Nations stands among the flowers and trees in the Garden of Gethsemane. The name Gethsemane *means "olive press," and ancient olive trees still grow here. The church has twelve mosaic domes. Inside, an altar has been built near the rock on which Jesus is thought to have prayed.*

Key words

foundation stone the first stone of a building; the rest of the building is constructed on top of it. Also known as cornerstone.

monks men who live together and devote their whole lives to serving God

laymen men who are not priests, who go to church and often help priests in their work

denominations different Christian groups

restoration mending something to make it look as it did before

nuns women who live together and devote their whole lives to serving God

votive candles These are lit and dedicated to the memory of someone or something special; prayers are said at the same time as the candles are lit.

Two Biblical women

Mary, Christ's mother, is a central figure in the Christian faith, but not much is known about her except that she came from Nazareth, a city in northern Israel. It is believed that Mary died in AD 63.

Another important figure in Christ's life was Mary Magdalene. A prostitute from the village of Magdala, she became a follower of Christ after he exorcised seven demons from her body. She was the first person to see Christ after his resurrection. She is often used as an example of Christ's willingness to associate with people considered outcasts by society.

Mosques of Jerusalem

All Muslims think of Jerusalem as the third holiest city after Mecca and Medina. Long ago, Muslim artists drew the world as a fish, with Mecca at its head, Medina at its tail, and the holy rock of Jerusalem on its back.

Many old friends of the Prophet Muhammad came to die and be buried in the city, for it was said that anyone who died in Jerusalem would be sure of a place in heaven.

The mosques in Jerusalem are used for prayer and learning, as they are all over the world. Each mosque has a leader, or imam, who leads the prayers when Muslims go to worship. They read parts of the Holy Koran, which tells the followers of Islam to be good, kind, and fair to all people.

The shiny Dome of the Rock was once made of real ▶ gold. It is now made of bronze-aluminum.

▼ This is one of the many tall minarets in Jerusalem.

Muslims worship five times each day. They are called to prayer by a muezzin, who, in a beautiful chanting voice, tells people that it is time to come to the mosque. He calls from a tower called a minaret. All Muslims must remove their shoes before entering the mosque, and there is a place in each mosque for worshipers to wash before they pray. The washing is done in a special way. Muslims stand, kneel, and bow down in a certain order as they say their prayers. All worshipers face the direction of the holy city of Mecca at prayer time. Each mosque has a small alcove or a stone slab that shows the right direction. This is called a mihrab.

El-Aqsa Mosque

The Dome of the Rock covers the sacred spot where the Holy Prophet Muhammad ascended to heaven with the archangel Gabriel. Nearby there is another building called the Dome of the Chain. It is a smaller copy of the big dome. In ancient times, fresh drinking water was carried from it to the worshipers in the other mosques around Jerusalem.

Close by stands the central mosque of Jerusalem. It was first built in AD 711, only 20 years after the Dome of the Rock, and is called el-Aqsa. It is here that pilgrims to the Dome gather for their prayers. On Friday, the most holy day of the week, Muslims can be seen making their ways through the markets for their midday worship.

The base for the present mosque was built on the site of the earlier one. But during the centuries, it has undergone many changes, because it lies on a fault line, or deep crack in the rocks. The mosque has often been shaken by the earth's movements.

There are a lot of other mosques throughout Jerusalem; some of them are quite small. Muslims pray at home, or indeed anywhere, if the time to pray has come and there is no mosque nearby. They often carry brightly colored prayer mats that are rolled

▲ *The Tomb of Joseph and the Mosque of Abraham*

out at prayer time. The mats are pointed toward the holy city of Mecca, and many of them have pictures of Mecca printed on or woven into them.

Islamic schools

Islamic schools have always been very important to Muslims. In Jerusalem there are some very old schools called *madarasa*, especially in the Muslim Quarter. One of these is Tashtimuriyya, which was built in 1382 by an imam, or religious leader, who also wanted the school to be a tomb!

El-Aqsa Mosque was built on the southern end of Temple Mount. It has been the scene of several disasters, including the murder of King Abdullah of Jordan
▼ *in 1951.*

Islamic Art

An important feature of most mosques is the art found outside and inside them. Islamic art is a mixture of Arabic, Persian, Syrian, and Egyptian styles. Many mosques are decorated with mosaics, pictures formed from bits of colored glass, wood, metal, or stone. Because the Koran forbids portraying people or animals in realistic form, mosaics are usually made up of intricate designs or flowerlike patterns. These designs can also be seen in the beautiful rugs woven by Muslim craftspeople.

Celebrations

Jewish Festivals

The Jewish New Year starts with Rosh Hoshanah, which means "New Year." It takes place in September or October. All Jews have a two-day holiday, followed by a ten-day fast when people do **penance** for their sins. Many people visit the Pool of Siloam, or any other slow-running stream, and shake their clothes to throw their sins into the water. The end of the ten-day fast marks another religious holiday called Yom Kippur, or the Day of Atonement. On this day, Jews go to the synagogue to pray for forgiveness.

The most exciting celebration is Sukkoth, or the Feast of the Tabernacles. This is a week-long festival that takes place in September or October. It is held to remember the life of the Jews in the desert after they fled from Egypt. Most families build little tents or booths, which are called *sukkoth* in Hebrew, to **commemorate** the 40 years that the Jews spent in the desert with no proper homes. Many people eat and sleep overnight in their tents. Some stay for the whole week.

Hanukkah usually takes place in December. This festival celebrates the capture of Jerusalem from the Seleucids in 165 BC and the reconsecration of the Temple. A huge, nine-branched candle called a menorah is lit by the Wailing Wall. As well, smaller ones are lighted in homes around the city.

Pesach, or Passover, is a feast of thanksgiving to God. It is celebrated in March or April. In a special meal cooked in pans kept just for this feast, Jews remember the last night that they were held captive in Egypt before they fled across the desert. On this night, a terrible **plague** swept through Egypt and killed many children. But the plague passed over the houses of all faithful Jews. So the Jewish children were saved and were free to leave Egypt with their parents.

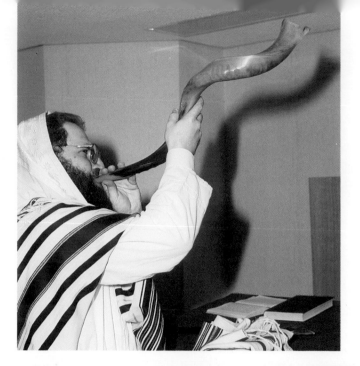

Top: The ram's horn in this picture is called a shofar. It is being blown at the ceremony of Rosh Hoshanah.

▲ This is an enormous booth for the feast of Sukkoth.

Christian festivals

Easter Sunday is the most important date in the Christian calendar. It celebrates Christ rising from the dead. The different Christian churches in Jerusalem hold special services.

In the Church of the Holy Sepulcher, the members of the Greek Orthodox church celebrate Easter with plenty of light. Christians call Jesus "the light of the world." So at Easter, pilgrims carry unlit candles and stand in the church. The church leader, or patriarch, enters bearing a torch. A flash of "holy fire" follows as all the candles are lit, and the church is set ablaze with light. The torch fire is then quickly sent on its way to

Greece, rather like the Olympic flame.

Christmas comes twice in Jerusalem. Western Christians celebrate it on December 25, while the Eastern churches have theirs on January 7. On this special occasion, many pilgrims go to Bethlehem, the birthplace of Christ, on the outskirts of Jerusalem. They take part in a mass in the Church of the Nativity. Afterward they visit a small room underneath the church. Here there is a silver star that marks the place where people think Jesus was born.

Muslim festivals

Many celebrations are centered around Ramadan, the ninth month of the Muslim year. The Muslim year begins during the month in which the Holy Prophet Muhammad was forced to flee from Mecca and travel to Medina for safety in AD 622. During Ramadan, Muslims do not eat or drink between dawn and dusk.

The month of fasting begins when the new moon first appears in the sky. The Holy Koran instructs Muslims not to eat each day until it is really dark.

The fast ends when the new moon of the following month rises. Then there is a feast called Id al-Fitr. Muslims celebrate the end of the fasting period by cooking rich foods and exchanging a sweet rice pudding with their friends and neighbors. Nearly everybody

▲ *These Muslim children have gone to the playground dressed in their best clothes for Id al-Fitr.*

wears new clothes and goes to the mosque, where they share special prayers and embrace one another. The children receive presents and money from their relatives.

Another celebration takes place two and a half months later. It is called Id al-Adha and marks the end of the period of pilgrimage to the holy city of Mecca that many Muslims undertake each year. Muslim families all over the world sacrifice an animal, usually a goat or a sheep. They are instructed by the Holy Koran to divide it into three parts. One part is given to the poor, one to family relatives, and the third is eaten by the family itself.

The silver star ▶

The birthplace of Christ ▼

Key words

penance an act that someone performs to show that he or she is sorry for doing wrong

commemorate to help people to remember a special time, usually with a ceremony or a celebration

plague a disease that is very dangerous and that spreads very quickly

Legends and traditions

The center of the world

Perhaps the most important tradition in Jerusalem is shared by both Jews and Muslims. Many Jews believe that the holy rock is the center of the world. It is thought that the Ark of the Covenant still lies underneath all the layers of ruins and rocks. Muslims also say that the rock is the center of the world, and that it lies on top of a palm tree growing in the River of Paradise, or heaven.

The walls of Jerusalem

The walls that surround Jerusalem have eight enormous gates. The Jaffa Gate enters the old city from West Jerusalem. Just inside it there is a small **grove** raised above the level of the street. There are a couple of cypress trees, a fig tree, and two graves surrounded by an iron fence. It is said that they are the graves of two Muslim architects who worked for Sultan Suleiman the Magnificent. These architects had the walls of Jerusalem rebuilt between 1538 and 1542.

This huge rock is the very top of Mount Moriah. King Solomon built his altar upon it, and Caliph Omar ibn-Kahtib had to remove tons of rubble before he could
▼ *find the rock in AD 638.*

But the deaths of the two architects are surrounded in mystery. Some people think that Suleiman had them killed because they forgot to include Mount Zion, with the much-honored tomb of King David, within the walls. Other people say that Suleiman was so pleased with the good job they had done that he had them killed so that they would never be able to build anything like it for anyone else!

The shoemaker thief

It is said that Jesus and two thieves were locked in a prison overnight as they waited for their crucifixion. This place has now been turned into a little chapel and made a part of the Church of the Holy Sepulcher. One of the thieves said that he was sorry for his sins as he hung on the cross. Jesus promised the thief that because he was sorry he would enter the kingdom of heaven to be with God. No one knows who this "good thief" was, and a number of legends have been told about him.

One says that the thief was a shoemaker. Mary, the mother of Jesus, and Joseph, his father, passed by the shoemaker's shop on their way to Egypt. They were escaping Herod the Great's command that all new-

▲ *Lions are carved on either side of Lions' Gate. It is said that Sultan Suleiman the Magnificent dreamed that he would be eaten by lions if he did not rebuild the walls of Jerusalem.*

born children should be killed. The shoemaker thief made the infant Jesus a pair of shoes, and this is why Christ forgave him his sins on the cross.

Tombs of Jerusalem

The Kidron Valley lies between Temple Mount and the Mount of Olives. Many ancient tombs have been found here. The two in the picture on the right have been named after Zachariah and Absalom, who were written about in the holy scriptures. People used to visit these "shrines" until they realized that they were in fact the tombs of two wealthy Jews. The tombs were built in the 2nd century AD, long after Zachariah and Absalom had died!

The tomb of Jesus

Some people say that Jesus Christ was not buried in the famous tomb inside the Church of the Holy Sepulcher, as many people believe. Instead they think that Jesus was buried in the Garden Tomb. This is a little **cavern** just off the Nablus Road. The English general Charles Gordon visited this place on his way to Egypt in 1883. He thought that it fitted better the descriptions he had read of Christ's tomb. There was also a skull-shaped hill nearby. General Gordon wondered if people had made a mistake. Could this be

▲ *These tombs were once thought to be those of Zachariah and Absalom.*

Christ's real tomb, he wondered? One night, Gordon had a **vision** that made him believe he was right. The tomb, with the surrounding land, was bought by English Christians, who still look after it and welcome visitors to it.

Key words

grove a group of trees

cavern a cave

vision a kind of dream

Just a dreamer?

Suleiman the Magnificent, a leader of the Ottoman Empire, ordered the walls around Jerusalem rebuilt after having a dream in which he was eaten by lions (a symbol of the Jewish nation) for refusing to rebuild the city. He was considered a fair and just ruler, although he once executed two of his own sons for disagreeing with him.

Art and architecture

Jerusalem's long and complicated history reflects many different styles of art and architecture. Some of the best works can be seen in the synagogues, churches, and mosques. Archaeologists have discovered many beautiful examples as they have dug beneath the city's old **foundations**. There are also fine examples of modern art and architecture and collections given to Jerusalem's museums by Jews who have bought paintings and sculptures from artists of many nationalities. The Jews, who have for centuries lived among other cultures all around the world, have brought different forms of art with them to Jerusalem.

The four Sephardic synagogues

There are four synagogues on Mishmerat Ha Kehuna Street that are all connected to one another. The oldest are the Elijah the Prophet and the Yohanan Ben Zakkai synagogues, which were built nearly 400 years ago. The entrance into the first synagogue, Elijah the Prophet, is through a sunken courtyard. All four buildings are low, because when they were built, the ruling Muslims did not allow any Jewish or Christian buildings to be taller than the Muslim ones in that area.

In the Elijah the Prophet Synagogue there is a beautiful carved wooden ark where the Torah **scrolls** are kept. The ark is also 400 years old but came from an Italian synagogue that was destroyed in the Second World War. The Yohanan Ben Zakkai Synagogue was built in traditional Sephardic style, with the seats arranged around the walls. There are iron rings in the ceiling, which once held oil lamps.

A Christian cathedral

The different Christian groups in Jerusalem have used many styles of art and architecture in their places of worship. One of the best examples is the Cathedral of Saint James in the Armenian Quarter. It was built where one of Jesus Christ's closest followers, or apostles, was killed. His name was James the Less.

Most of the cathedral was built by the 12th century AD. Near the front door there is an ancient wooden board. When the Muslim Turks ruled Jerusalem, they did not allow church bells to be rung. Christians did not know when it was time to go to the cathedral to worship. So this board was put up and beaten loudly so that everyone could hear.

▼ *Lamps hanging from the ceiling of the Yohanan Ben Zakkai Synagogue*

The Persian tiles on the Dome of the Rock

This beautifully decorated page from the Holy Koran was displayed in the Moshed Shrine Library during the World of Islam Festival.

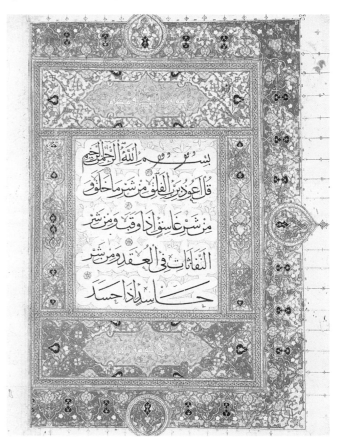

Inside the cathedral, the floors are covered with bold, brightly colored carpets. The pillars are decorated with Spanish tiles. There is a large dome with a tower in the shape of a **hexagon**. One of the shrines has a door decorated with tortoiseshell and shiny **mother-of-pearl**. Outside, the cathedral has a courtyard with a beautiful fountain.

Islamic art

Muslim designers and artists are forbidden by the Holy Koran to make either human or animal forms in their works of art. So they create designs in beautiful and often very complicated patterns of **geometrical** shapes, flowers, or Arabic script.

The Dome of the Rock and el-Aqsa Mosque are good examples of Islamic art.
The Dome was built originally in AD 691 by Caliph Abd el-Malik. The **octagonal** building, though, is from the 13th century. It contains the original mosaics and beautiful marble and stonework, which people think were created during the reign of Saladin in the 12th century.

Beautiful mosques

El-Aqsa Mosque was built originally by Caliph Abd el-Malik's son, el-Walid, to commemorate the Holy Prophet Muhammad's night journey to heaven. Seven arches form the entrance porch of this beautiful mosque, and mosaics decorate the ceiling. The tall columns are frosted with marble. The mosque was built to face Mecca, and richly colored stained-glass windows pierce the southern wall near the mihrab. Patterned carpets brighten the floor.

Between the Dome of the Rock and el-Aqsa Mosque there is a water fountain called el-Kas, or "the Cup." Here, Muslims sit on stone seats to cleanse themselves before they go to pray in the mosque. Muslim designers often made breathtaking gardens, with water fountains, pools, shade trees, and paths in geometrical shapes.

Near el-Aqsa Mosque are the Islamic Museum, the Dome of Joseph, which was built by Saladin in 1191, and the Women's Mosque. The museum displays Islamic art and beautifully written verses of the Holy Koran on manuscripts and on shiny glazed titles. The Women's Mosque is decorated in cool, peaceful shades of blue.

Ancient art in Jerusalem

The Roman rulers destroyed the Second Temple of the Jews in AD 70, and with it most of Jerusalem. But in 1970, an archaeologist found a group of mansions, or grand houses, built during the rule of Herod the Great. So we now know how some of the dwellings looked in the first century AD. He also found what is now called the Burnt House. In it there were mosaics, **frescoes**, stone tables, sunken baths, covered courtyards, rooms with plaster decorations, fine glassware, stone jars, and many other beautiful things. It was the house of someone very religious, as there were private *mikvehs*, or baths for special religious washing. It is thought that the house belonged to a wealthy high priest.

New art in Jerusalem

The Knesset is Israel's flat-roofed parliament building, where the government passes laws and makes decisions. It is a good example of modern art and architecture. The Session Hall, where parliament is held, has three magnificent **tapestries** in it designed by a famous artist, Marc Chagall. They show the creation of humankind, the flight of the Jews from Egypt, and Jerusalem itself.

Outside the building is an **eternal** flame that burns in honor of Israel's soldiers killed in several wars. **Wrought-iron** work surrounds the flame. The outer gates of the Knesset are the work of the Israeli artist David Polombo. Opposite the main gate is a huge bronze menorah, the nine-branched candle-holder that is Israel's national symbol. The menorah's nine branches represent different stages in the history of the Jews, from Moses to the present day.

◀ *These are the remains of the houses built during the 1st century AD below Temple Mount. There was going to be a Jewish college, or yeshiva, built on top of these ruins, but they were too important to be covered up.*

▲ The Dead Sea Scrolls lie inside a white, dome-shaped building called the Shrine of the Book.

▲ This brightly colored wall just outside Jerusalem is a good example of street art. Beyond it are modern apartments that have been built in West Jerusalem.

Israel Museum

This museum was built in West Jerusalem in 1965. It contains not only works of art by Jews, but also works created by those of other faiths and from other nations. One of the most important things to see is the white, domelike structure, the Shrine of the Book, which holds the Dead Sea Scrolls. These scrolls are ancient writings found in 1947 in a desert cave. They are thought to contain records of the Jewish uprising against the Romans between AD 132 and 135. There are also pieces of the books of the Bible. The shape of the white dome that surrounds them is the same as the clay jar in which the scrolls were found. The museum also holds examples of traditional wedding dress and art used in Jewish ceremonies.

Key words

foundations the bases on which buildings are constructed

scrolls rolled-up paper or other material for writing on

hexagon a shape with six sides and six angles

mother-of-pearl the shiny, colored inside of a shell

geometrical shapes, such as circles, squares, and triangles

octagon a shape with eight sides and eight angles

frescoes wall paintings made on damp plaster

tapestries pictures made out of thousands of sewn stitches

eternal without an end

wrought iron iron that is shaped and curved into patterns

Dinnertime in Jerusalem

Nothing reflects Jerusalem's cultural and racial mix better than its food. As people moved to the city from other countries, they added new foodstuffs, recipes, and traditions to local cooking. Religion plays an important part in the diets of both Jews and Muslims.

Kosher

Many Jews eat only kosher food. When food is kosher, it means that the ingredients have been prepared according to the laws set down in the Torah. Kosher law also prevents Jews from eating pork, shellfish, or **game**. Meat and dairy products cannot be eaten together, either. So a cheeseburger cannot be bought in West Jerusalem, where the people are mostly Jewish. Neither can Jews put milk in their after-dinner coffee if they have just eaten meat.

▲ *Israel produces all kinds of fruits. Here you can see a well-stocked fruit stall in Yehuda covered market in West Jerusalem.*

Halal

Muslims eat only *"halal"* meat. Like kosher food, the meat must be prepared according to religious law, as set out in the Koran. The law also prevents Muslims from eating pork and from drinking alcohol.

This falafel bar is only one of many kinds of snack bars ▼ *in Jerusalem.*

Breakfast

Breakfast in Jerusalem is usually a big meal. This could include eggs, fresh fruit, pickled vegetables, olives, sliced tomatoes, yogurt, and cheese. All this is washed down with a lot of coffee and fruit juice. Some people also eat hummus, a delicious paste made from crushed chick peas, oil, and garlic.

Lunch

Lunch is the main meal of the day for many people in Jerusalem. Smoked turkey is popular with the Jews. It is served with pickled vegetables and followed by dessert.

Muslim Arabs prefer lamb dishes. They have many different ones but the most popular is probably *shwarma*. This is a kebab of lamb, or lamb cooked on a metal spike. Other popular dishes are fried lambs' brains and stuffed lambs' hearts. Salads are eaten with most of these meals.

Dinner

Most people in Jerusalem have a small dinner. It is usually a simple salad or sandwiches. If they are eating in a restaurant, however, people usually have a large meal followed by dessert. The Jews from Central Europe have brought many European sweet dishes with them. So have the Muslims from other Middle Eastern countries. The most popular of these is called *baklava*. This is a flaky pastry case filled with ground nuts and honey. Muslims also eat *mohalabiyeh*, which is a sweet cake made with milk and sweet-smelling rose water.

Snacks

During the day, a lot of Jerusalemites eat falafel. These are spiced chick pea balls served in pita bread. They are sold from little **kiosks** on the streets. Some kiosks also sell chilled fruit and vegetable juices. Many bars serve different kinds of coffee, often flavored with cardamom seeds. The hot weather

▲ *Hummus is a delicious and popular snack. Here you can see someone dipping pita bread into it.*

makes it necessary for people in Jerusalem to drink frequently.

Midnight feast

No one needs to go hungry in Jerusalem late at night. Street sellers are out until all hours, tempting people with sweets and cakes. One of the most delicious is *kadaifi*, which is made from shredded wheat, pistachio nuts, and honey, all baked in the shape of a nest.

Key words

game animals or birds that are hunted for their meat

kiosks street stalls

The Seder Supper

Food is especially important at the seder, the traditional dinner held by Jews during Passover. At the seder, people eat boiled eggs, matzo (unleavened bread), *haroset* (a mixture of nuts, apples, sugar, and wine), and *maror* (a bitter vegetable similar to horseradish).

Important events in the history of Jerusalem

The following are some important events with the dates on which they occurred:

BC BEFORE THE BIRTH OF CHRIST

3000 First evidence of settlements on the site of Jerusalem

2150–1550 The age of the Patriarchs: Abraham, Isaac, and Jacob

1550–1250 Hebrews go to Egypt. Moses returns to Canaan with them and receives the Torah, or Law, on Mount Sinai. Hebrews now known as the Israelites and spend the next 40 years traveling to their Promised Land

1025 Saul becomes first king of Israel

1000 David, now king of Israel, conquers Jebus, known afterward as Jerusalem. He brings the Ark of the Covenant to the city. Jerusalem becomes the new religious center as well as the political capital

968 Solomon becomes king of Israel and builds the First Temple to the Lord on Mount Moriah

933 Death of Solomon. Kingdom is divided: to the north is Israel; to the south, Judah, with its capital, Jerusalem

722 Destruction of the Kingdom of Israel by the Assyrians. Most of the Jews are sent from the kingdom. Judah under influence of Assyria

701 Jerusalem resists attack by Assyrians

587 Babylonians capture Jerusalem and the Temple is destroyed. Jews are exiled to Babylon

515 Persians take over the Kingdom of Judah. Many Jews are allowed back in Jerusalem. The Second Temple is built

457 The scribe Ezra returns from Babylon and reforms the Jewish religion

333 Persian Empire is defeated by Alexander the Great, ruler of Greek Empire. Judah, now known as Judea, comes under his rule

300 Jewish Bible translated into Greek

198 Seleucids take over Judea, but treat the Jewish community well

167 Beginning of Maccabean Revolt

165 Judah the Maccabee enters the Temple and rededicates it

165–63 Jewish leaders expand the Kingdom of Judea

63 Romans take over Judea and rule for next 400 years

37 Herod the Great made king of Judea, but has to fight to claim his throne in Jerusalem. Is much hated, even though he rebuilds the Temple

5 or 6 Birth of Jesus Christ in Bethlehem, Judea

4 Death of Herod the Great

AD   AFTER THE BIRTH OF CHRIST

29 Jesus celebrates Passover in Jerusalem, is arrested, tried, and crucified

66 The Jewish war against the Romans

70 Romans overcome Jewish rebels and destroy the Second Temple

132 Jews fight Romans to stop Emperor Hadrian from making Jerusalem a city for many gods

135 Hadrian defeats Jews and builds a city for the gods. Jerusalem now called Aelia Capitolina, and Judea known as Palestina

325 Emperor Constantine makes Jerusalem Christian and part of his Byzantine Empire

500 Babylonian Talmud completed

614 Persian invasion of Jerusalem. Many churches destroyed

622 Muhammad's flight from Mecca to Medina. Islamic religion is born and a Muslim empire grows

628 Persians defeated. Byzantines again rule in Jerusalem

632 Death of the Holy Prophet Muhammad. Muslim Arab Empire now ruled by religious, political, and military leader known as the caliph

638 Byzantine Jerusalem taken over by Muslim caliph Omar

691 Caliph Abd el-Malik builds Dome of the Rock in Jerusalem

775–1071 Jerusalem ruled by three different Muslim empires

1099 The First Crusade. Jerusalem taken and most Jews and Muslims massacred

1187 Christian armies of Second Crusade defeated by Muslim leader Saladin. Crusaders leave the Holy Land

1191 Third Crusade arrives and Christians gain some land, but never properly hold on to Jerusalem, which by now is not the great city it once was

1270 The seventh and last Crusade

1291 Muslim Egyptian Mamluks conquer Palestine and take over Jerusalem

1492 Jews driven out of Spain. Many later settle in Jerusalem

1516 Jewish community in Palestine begins to grow again

1538 Suleiman the Magnificent rebuilds walls of Jerusalem

1700 Ashkenazim, or East European Jews, arrive in Jerusalem

1799 Palestine invaded by Emperor Napoleon Bonaparte of France

1832 Ibrahim Pasha, a Muslim from Egypt, takes control of Palestine

1840 Egyptians pushed out of Palestine by Turkey, helped by countries such as France and Great Britain, which gained religious and economic strength in this area

1882 Arrival of first modern Jewish settlers

1918 Jerusalem taken over by the British at the end of the First World War

1948 Jews declare the State of Israel, but the Old City of Jerusalem remains with the Muslim Palestinians of Jordan

1967 Israel gains Jerusalem in the Six Day War

1973 Israel fights off Egyptian and Syrian armies on the Jewish festival of Yom Kippur, the Day of Atonement

1987 Intafadeh, or Palestinian uprising begins

Further Reading

Keene, Michael. *Being a Muslim*. North Pomfret, Vermont: Trafalgar Square, 1987.

Kuskin, Karla. *Jerusalem, Shining Still*. New York: HarperCollins, 1987.

Lawless, Richard. *The Middle East Since 1945*. North Pomfret, Vermont: Trafalgar Square, 1989.

Lynch, Patricia. *Christianity*. New York: Facts on File, 1991.

Morris, Ann. *When Will the Fighting Stop? A Child's View of Jerusalem*. New York: Atheneum, 1990.

Webber-Doyle, Terrence. *Tug-of-War: Peace Through Understand Conflict*. Ojai, California: Atrium, 1990.

Index